Ham and Chicken
Do Brazil

By Kimberly Naylor
Illustrated by Delaney Swift

Olá! My name is Chicken
and this guy is Ham.
Today we go to Brazil
to discover a new land.

FACTS ABOUT BRAZIL:

1. 5th largest nation in the world
2. Capital City: Brasilia
3. Only country in <u>South America</u> that speaks <u>Portuguese</u>.
   Most others speak Spanish.
4. Money: Brazilian real
5. Host of Soccer World Cup 2014
6. Host of Summer Olympics 2016

Brazil's flag

3

Let's learn something new about our <u>destination</u>. We think it will help us have a great vacation!

Only <u>natives</u> lived there
way back in the day
until some <u>Europeans</u>
went over to stay.

The year was 1500
when <u>Cabral</u> sailed on over.
"This place is mine now.
<u>Portugal</u> is taking over."

"I really like this place.
I think I'll stay. I should.
We'll make loads of money
selling this brazilwood."

This tree was very <u>valuable</u>.
Its wood was highly famed.
Brazilwood was the way by which
Brazil got its name.

6

They chopped down these trees for a reason-
to make sawdust and wood shreds.
They mixed them with hot liquids to make
dyes of yellows, oranges, and reds.

For over 300 years
the <u>Portuguese</u> stayed,
also making money in
the gold and rubber trade.

7

By 1822,
Brazil's time had come
to get out from under
the <u>Portuguese</u> thumb.

They fought for their <u>independence</u>
and freedom was surely won.
Brazil became its own country
and <u>Portugal's</u> rule was done.

But to this day Brazilians
still speak <u>Portuguese</u>.
"Obrigado" ("o-bree-god-o") is thank you
and "por favor" ("poor-fuh-vore") is please.

We'll start at the Amazon, a river and jungle of worth.
It's the most <u>biodiverse</u> place on earth.

Through the north of Brazil,
this river keeps flowing;
from <u>Peru</u> to the <u>Atlantic</u>,
is the way that it's going.

It holds the most water,
more than most combined.
When you stand on the edge,
it's hard to see the other side.

The Amazon has more water
than the <u>Nile</u> plus the <u>Yangtze</u>.
It even has more water than
if you add the <u>Mississippi</u>.

11

Parts of the river are dark,
while others are milky white.
The "meeting of the waters"
is really quite the sight.

But be careful of what swims below.
There are fish called piranha... and they bite!

To find these fish with sharp teeth,
you don't have to go far.
Go fish right off the dock.
They prefer steak tartare.

Dolphins also swim here.
"Boto" is their nickname.
They are pink! Can you believe it?
Their color brought them great fame!

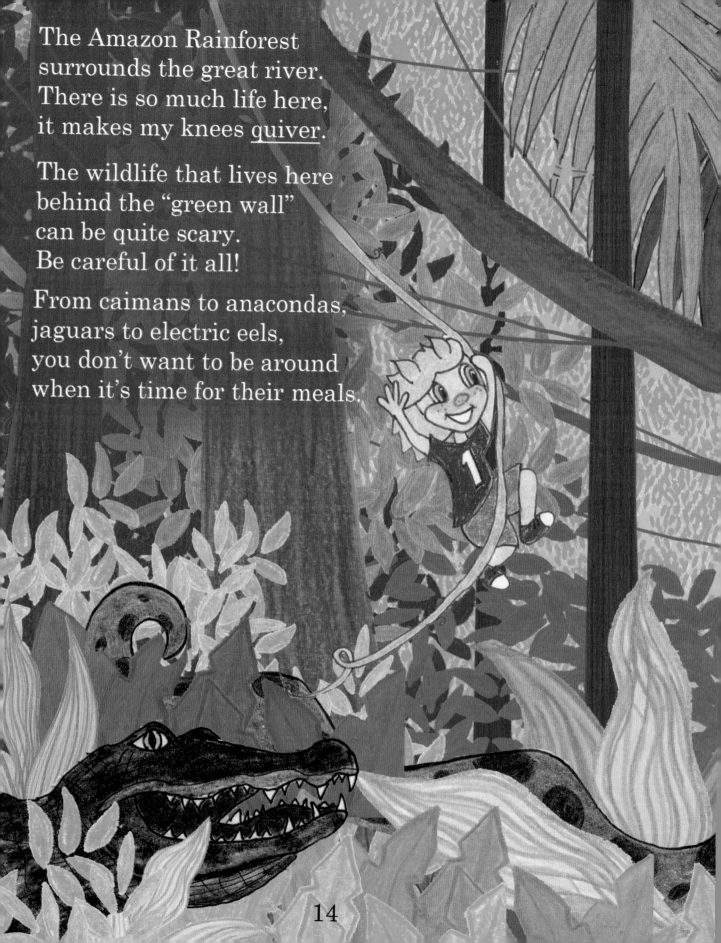

The Amazon Rainforest
surrounds the great river.
There is so much life here,
it makes my knees <u>quiver</u>.

The wildlife that lives here
behind the "green wall"
can be quite scary.
Be careful of it all!

From caimans to anacondas,
jaguars to electric eels,
you don't want to be around
when it's time for their meals.

14

15

On the border with <u>Argentina</u>,
shaped in a big horseshoe,
the widest waterfall in the world
is found at Iguazu.(Ee-gwa-soo)

Brazil

Argentina

TRAVEL BUG

Hike through the jungle there.
Walk along the falls too.
Take a ferry across
and see Argentina's view.

17

Here we are in Rio!
First, let's go to the beaches-
a beautiful stretch of sand and water
as far as the eye reaches.

Why are those people
dressed in white on the sand?
They have all come with
white flowers in their hands.

18

They throw the flowers to the sea
as an act of <u>devotion</u>.
Once a year they pay respect
to the goddess of the ocean.

They say this brings good luck.
It is their <u>tradition</u>.
So if you come on New Year's Eve,
you too can do some wishin'!

Once a year they throw this party.
All around the music booms.
With glitter and sparkles everywhere,
they wear such colorful costumes.

20

Carnaval

Maybe we should try the dance school.
They can give us some tips
on how to dance the <u>samba</u>
and how to shake our hips.

We can dance in the streets
in a <u>samba</u> parade
all day and all night
until the music fades.

Here we are at Corcovado.
There's a 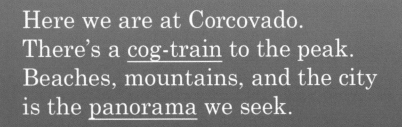cog-train to the peak.
Beaches, mountains, and the city
is the panorama we seek.

Look up to the tippy top,
but do not be alarmed.
Christ the Redeemer
stands tall open armed.

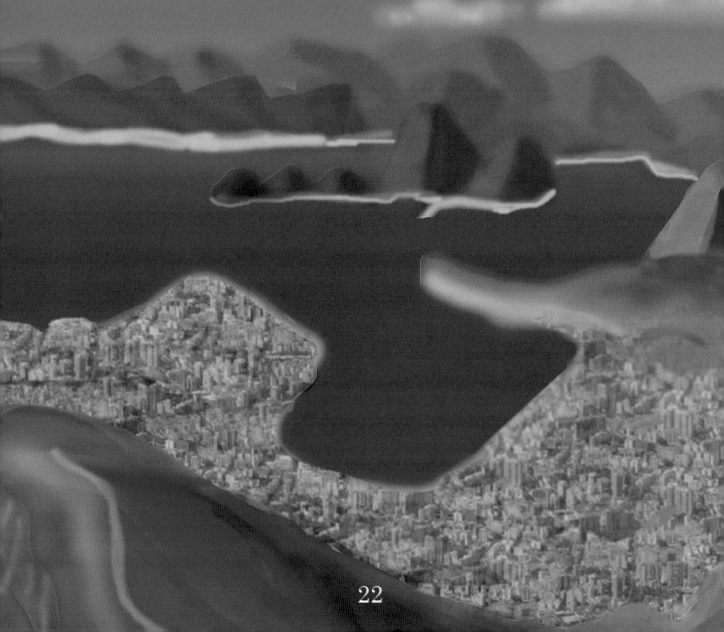

Looking out over Rio,
He has the very best views.
You can see them for yourself.
There are stairs that you can use.

Climb all the steps to the viewing deck
but make sure to wear some good shoes.

Speaking of views,
here's something to try.
Jump off a mountain
and into the sky.
With the help of a hang glider,
you too can fly!

Let's go to Sugarloaf Mountain;
it's really not that far.
Try to say it in <u>Portuguese</u>...
"pow de ah-soo-car." (Pao de Acucar)

Hop on in, we can take a cable car!

This smaller mountain
is shaped like a cake.
It still offers terrific views.
Oh the pictures you can take!

Over here, I'm open!
Quick! Make your pass!
Brazilian soccer players
are considered world-class!

The fans are truly <u>fanatic</u>.
The stadiums are always filled.
To be here at a game now,
it's so exciting! I'm thrilled!

26

Almost a religion
instead of just a sport,
the soccer team of Brazil
might be its biggest export.

27

Over by Natal,
you can be the biggest boaster
if you can surf the dunes
fast like a roller coaster.

We can take rides in buggies
driven by a local guide.
They go fast over every turn.
Hang on tight when you ride!

Next we're off to the islands.
They are to the northeast.
Fernando de Noronha!
For the eyes, it's a feast!

There is a <u>marine</u> <u>refuge</u>
on this <u>archipelago</u>.
And for this very reason,
not many people can go.

We are lucky to be here
but now school's in session.
Let's learn how to go diving.
Let's take a scuba lesson.

Barracuda, sea turtles-
they are everywhere.
The coral reef is so colorful,
but be sure to take care.

Dolphins and albatrosses
all live in this biome.
We must help to protect it.
They call this place home.

Before we leave this country,
before we are through,
we'd like to try a couple of things,
two things that are new.

Can you guess what we're doing?
No? Take a second glance.
It's a type of <u>martial arts</u>-
a mix of fighting and break dance.

If given a chance to learn capoeira (cap-o-where-uh),
do not miss your chance.

Can you guess what this is?
Another thing I want to try
is a bright purple fruit.
Want some? Don't be shy!

Mmm, that's good!
It's called acai (ah-sigh-ee).
It's the perfect healthy snack
and boy is it tasty!

Tchau, we must leave you.
We got our vacation fill.
We are so glad you joined us
in beautiful Brazil.

But there's something to remember
and please don't forget:
The more you learn of our world,
the smaller it can get.

The places can look different,
the people not like you,
but we all want the same in life:
Peace, Love, and Happiness- to name a few.

So when you go off traveling
to an amazing destination
respect the people, culture, and land
and have an awesome vacation!

Glossary

archipelago: a large group of islands

Argentina: a country in South America, see map 2

Atlantic: Atlantic Ocean, 2nd largest ocean in the world, see maps 1 and 2

biodiverse: many different kinds of plants and/or animals

biome: an area where certain plants and animals live under a certain
        kind of weather

Cabral: Pedro Alvares Cabral, an explorer from Portugal who is said to
         have discovered Brazil

cog-train: a special kind of train whose tracks allow the train to go up
            and down steep mountains

destination: the place that you are going to

devotion: a strong feeling of love or loyalty

Europeans: people from Europe, see map 1

export: something that is sold to another country

fanatic: extremely excited about a particular sport, thing, or belief

independence: freedom

marine: in and around the sea

Mississippi: a major river in the United States, flowing through a total
    of 10 states. Also a state in the United States.

natives: a group of people who are born in a certain place

Nile: a river in Africa, the longest river in the world

panorama: a wide view in all directions

Peru: a country in South America, see map 2

Portugal: a country in Europe, see map 1

Portuguese: things (like a language or people) from Portugal

quiver: to shake

refuge: a place of shelter or protection

samba: a kind of music and dance that has been performed by Brazilians
    for a long time

South America: a continent, see maps 1 and 2

tartare: not cooked

tradition: the stories and acts that have been celebrated by a group of people
    for a long time

valuable: worth a lot of money, important, useful

Yangtze: a river in China, the longest river in Asia

Map 1.

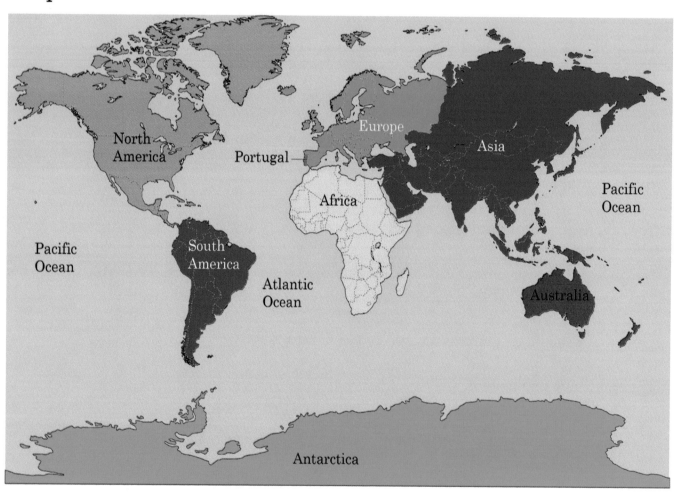

The continents of the world

Map 2.

South America

Acknowledgments:

Thank you to Samantha Shannon whose simple but sage advice went a long way, Meredith Tennant for your editorial skills, and the many friends who gave encouragement and honest opinions.
Thank you Mom...your love of birthday and Christmas card poems has been an inspiration!
Thank you to my very talented cousin, Delaney Swift. You went on this journey with me even though we had no idea where it would go. You might be the most patient person I know.
Thank you Nick, Nicholas, Adria, and Saltydog...I love you all infinity times infinity.
-KN

Thank you to my family for being supportive and encouraging me to develop my artistic abilities. Especially Damon, you are super great!
Thank you to my canine assistants Mason and Sammy for logging many hours napping by my side.
Thank you to my cousin Kim for the opportunity to dive into the deep end head first.
-DS

Travel Bug Press 2016
ISBN: 978-0-9979493-0-8

ISBN 978-0-9979493-0-8

9 780997 949308 >